SRI LANKA 2016 HUMAN RIGHTS REPORT

EXECUTIVE SUMMARY

Sri Lanka is a constitutional, multiparty republic with a freely elected government. In January 2015, voters elected President Maithripala Sirisena to a five-year term. The Parliament shares power with the president. August 2015 parliamentary elections resulted in a coalition government between the two major political parties. Both elections were free and fair.

Civilian authorities generally maintained effective control over the security forces; however, there were continued reports that police and security forces sometimes acted independently.

· The most significant human rights problems were incidents of arbitrary arrest, lengthy detention, surveillance, and harassment of civil society activists, journalists, members of religious minorities, and persons viewed as sympathizers of the Liberation Tigers of Tamil Eelam (LTTE).

Other human rights problems included abuse of power and reports of torture by security services. Severe prison overcrowding and lack of due process remained problems, as did some limits on freedoms of assembly and association, corruption, physical and sexual abuse of women and children, and trafficking in persons. Discrimination against women, persons with disabilities, and persons based on sexual orientation continued, and limits on workers' rights and child labor also remained problems.

Impunity for crimes committed during and following the armed conflict continued, particularly in cases of killings, torture, sexual violence, corruption, and other human rights abuses. The government made incremental progress on addressing impunity for violations of human rights. The government took some steps to arrest and detain a limited number of military, police, and other officials implicated in old and new cases, including the killing of parliamentarians and the abductions and suspected killings of journalists and private citizens.

Section 1. Respect for the Integrity of the Person, Including Freedom from:

a. Arbitrary Deprivation of Life and other Unlawful or Politically Motivated Killings

There were several reports that the government or its agents committed arbitrary or unlawful killings. On October 20, police killed two Jaffna University students near a police checkpoint in Jaffna, sparking protests across the country. Police arrested five police officers the following day in connection with the incident, and the president announced the police would conduct a full, impartial investigation into the students' deaths.

In September the Asian Human Rights Commission reported that police arrested a man in Nuwara Eliya for possession of alcohol without a permit. The man died while in custody. The police claimed that the victim committed suicide. The Asian Human Rights Commission stated that the victim's family members saw the police beat the victim prior to his death. In response to this incident, the minister for law and order stated that the ministry would install cameras in cells in order to prevent such occurrences. The Criminal Investigation Division of the police initiated an investigation into the incident, which continued at year's end.

On December 24, the courts acquitted five of the six persons indicted by the attorney general in July on accusations of killing Tamil National Alliance parliamentarian and prominent human rights advocate Nadaraja Raviraj in 2006. Three of the accused men were former naval officers. In May the courts ordered the arrest of former senior deputy inspector general of police Anura Senanayake and inspector Sumith Perera for their alleged role in attempting to cover up the May 2010 murder of rugby player Wasim Thajudeen. Members of the previous government were suspected of ordering the murder and involving Senanayake and Perera. Investigations into this case had stalled under the previous government but resumed in February 2015. In October a magistrate court ruled that the 2013 killing of three protesters in Rathupaswala was a crime. The protesters had demanded the removal of a factory, which they believed was polluting the drinking water. Army officers fired upon the crowd, killing three persons and injuring several others. There was no movement toward prosecution by year's end.

b. Disappearances

There were no reports of politically motivated disappearances.

The issue of involuntary disappearances during the war remained unresolved and in a July report, the UN Working Group on Enforced or Involuntary Disappearances (WGEID) stated, "enforced disappearances have been used in a massive and systematic way in Sri Lanka for many decades to suppress political dissent, counterterrorist activities, or in the internal armed conflict." WGEID noted the number of outstanding cases of enforced or involuntary disappearances at 5,750. In August the government passed a bill to establish an Office of Missing Persons to investigate disappearances but the office was yet to be established by year's end.

There was progress in the case of Prageeth Eknaligoda, a journalist and cartoonist for *Lanka-e-news*, who disappeared in 2010 just before the presidential election. On August 23, the Criminal Investigation Department cleared Eknaligoda of any links to the LTTE or criminal gangs, a claim that was popularly used to justify his disappearance. The police arrested 13 persons, including nine military intelligence officers, in 2015 and early 2016 in connection with Eknaligoda's disappearance. A court granted bail to all 13 suspects in November, after holding them for almost one year without indictment.

In 2013 National Water Supply and Drainage Board construction workers discovered a mass grave in Mannar District. Subsequent investigations uncovered at least 83 skeletal remains before the government halted the excavations. The former Rajapaksa government publicly blamed either the LTTE or the Indian peacekeeping force for any killings. In August police recovered five bone fragments and a tooth from an abandoned well near this mass grave. There reportedly were plans to conduct a forensic examination of these remains, although foreign forensic experts familiar with the case expressed concerns that the excavation methods used by the government possibly rendered meaningful forensic analysis impossible. On November 7, a Mannar court directed complainants to contact forensic experts to determine their willingness to test the samples and provide a recommendation to the court during the next hearing on January 15, 2017.

c. Torture and Other Cruel, Inhuman, or Degrading Treatment or Punishment

The law makes torture a punishable offense and mandates a sentence of not less than seven years' and not more than 10 years' imprisonment. There were credible reports that police and military forces abducted, tortured, and sexually abused citizens. The Prevention of Terrorism Act (PTA) allows courts to admit as evidence any statements made by the accused at any time, and provides no exception for confessions extracted by torture.

The Human Rights Commission of Sri Lanka's (HRCSL) report to the UN Committee Against Torture (UNCAT) review published in October indicated that the HRCSL received 208 allegations of torture by state actors from January 1 to August 31. According to the report, the HRCSL was in the process of establishing a Custodial Violations Unit in its Investigations and Inquiries Division to build specialized capacity about custodial issues, and to expedite investigations and inquiries into such complaints. The HRCSL also was in the process of establishing a Rapid Response Unit to help prevent torture by mandating visits to police stations and detention centers immediately after representatives of an arrested person filed a complaint against the state. In June, Foreign Minister Mangala Samaraweera publicly criticized the culture of torture among security forces and affirmed the government's commitment to eradicate torture. The government arrested several members of the armed services and political class suspected in unsolved cases, some more than a decade old.

In May the UN special rapporteur on torture and other cruel, inhuman and degrading treatment or punishment and the UN special rapporteur on the independence of judges and lawyers visited the country and delivered preliminary observations and recommendations. They concluded that torture remained a common practice in both criminal and national security cases and that the criminal justice system facilitated the use of torture to extract confessions to build cases. They stated that police investigators used torture and ill treatment routinely.

In July the government established a committee to visit, examine, and take preventive measures on allegations of torture. The committee included experts on torture prevention from the Bar Association of Sri Lanka, the Attorney General's Department, and senior members of the police.

The constitution prohibits torture and cruel treatment. In an October report submitted to the UNCAT, however, the International Truth and Justice Project reported seven cases of torture and/or other cruel, inhuman and degrading treatment by security forces. All of the reported victims were men of Tamil origin.

In January, according to HRCSL office in Kandy, police unlawfully arrested a woman on murder charges while she attempted to file a complaint of the same murder with the Nawalapitiya police station. Police allegedly tortured and sexually assaulted the woman and forced her to drink her own urine. She remained in police custody as of December 1 because she was unable to afford the approved bail conditions.

Several released former combatants reported torture or mistreatment, including sexual harassment and abuse by government officials while in rehabilitation centers and after their release. Excessive use of force against civilians by police and security officials also remained a problem.

Prison and Detention Center Conditions

Prison conditions were poor due to old infrastructure, overcrowding, and shortage of sanitary and other basic facilities. A few of the larger prisons had their own hospitals, but only a medical unit staffed the majority. Authorities transferred prisoners requiring medical care in smaller prisons to the closest local hospital for treatment. In September 2015, the government appointed a task force to analyze the legal and judicial causes of prison overcrowding. The International Committee of the Red Cross provided technical and logistical support to the task force, advised on international best practices for prison systems, and helped formulate strategies for prison reform.

Physical Conditions: Gross overcrowding was a problem; the commissioner of prisons estimated that on average the prison population exceeded the system's capacity by 50 percent. Authorities sometimes held juveniles and adults together. Authorities often held pretrial detainees and convicted prisoners together. In many prisons, inmates reportedly slept on concrete floors, and prisons often lacked natural light or sufficient ventilation.

The commissioner of prisons reported 74 total deaths of prisoners in custody as of November 29. The majority of deaths were due to natural causes; there were also three suicides.

Administration: There were no ombudspersons to handle prisoner complaints, however superintendents of prisons can accept complaints and prisoners may submit anonymous complaints into complaint boxes at the prisons. The HRCSL, the International Committee of the Red Cross (ICRC), magistrates, and independent monitors appointed by the Ministry of Prison Reforms may all accept complaints from prisoners. The law mandates that magistrates visit prisons once a month to monitor conditions and hold private interviews with prisoners, but this rarely occurred because the backlog of cases in courts made it difficult for magistrates to schedule such visits. The HRCSL reported it received some credible allegations of mistreatment reported by prisoners, but the Ministry of Prison Reforms reported it did not receive any complaints.

Independent Monitoring: The Prison Welfare Society was the primary domestic organization conducting visits to prisoners and has a mandate in regulations to examine the conditions of detention for prisoners and negotiate their complaints with the individual prison superintendents and the commissioners of prison.

Improvements: The Prison Department sought to address overcrowding by moving several prisons out of urban areas into more spacious, rural locations. For example, the Department moved Jaffna Prison outside of the city.

d. Arbitrary Arrest or Detention

The law prohibits arbitrary arrest and detention, but such incidents occurred, although at a decreased rate compared with 2015.

Role of the Police and Security Apparatus

Under the Ministry of Law and Order, the Police Service is responsible for maintaining internal security. The army is responsible for external security, but according to the criminal procedure code, the military may be called upon to handle specific domestic security responsibilities. The president is the minister of defense but the secretary of defense had daily operational responsibility over the army, navy, and air force. The nearly 6,000-member paramilitary Special Task Force falls under the Ministry of Law and Order, although joint operations with military units in previous years called into question the task force's chain of command.

Civilian authorities generally maintained effective control over the security forces, but the military and police continued to harass civilians with impunity. The Ministry of Law and Order is responsible for examining security force killings and evaluation of whether they were justifiable. According to civil society, military intelligence operatives conducted domestic surveillance operations and harassed or intimidated members of civil society in conjunction with, or independent of, police.

Impunity for conflict era abuses also persisted. Prosecutions for abuses committed by the security forces and police are rare, as are prosecutions for government corruption and malfeasance. There is no internal mechanism to investigate security force abuses and the only recourse is filing a case with the Supreme Court. The HRCSL and courts can investigate such abuses, but civil society organizations widely assert impunity is embedded in the system and the courts are reluctant to take action against security forces. The government implemented human rights training in the defense academy to increase respect for human rights and also allowed the ICRC to conduct training, but there is no systematic or standardized training.

The military continued to engage in nonmilitary economic activities in the north and east, including farming, fishing, and tourism.

Arrest Procedures and Treatment While in Detention

The Criminal Procedure Code allows police to make an arrest without a warrant for certain offenses such as homicide, theft, robbery, and rape. In other cases, police made arrests pursuant to arrest warrants that judges and magistrates issued based on evidence. By law authorities are required to inform an arrested person of the reason for the arrest and arraign that person before a magistrate within 24 hours for minor crimes, 48 hours for some grave crimes, and 72 hours for crimes covered by the PTA. In practice, however, more time regularly elapsed before detained persons appeared before a magistrate, particularly in PTA cases. For bailable offenses as characterized under the Bail Act, instead of arraignment in court the police can release suspects within 24 hours of detention on a written undertaking and require them to report to the courts on a specified date. Suspects accused of committing bailable offenses are entitled to bail but suspects accused of nonbailable offenses can only be awarded bail based on the magistrate's discretion. The Bail Act states no person should be held in custody prior to conviction and sentencing for more than 12 months without special exemptions, but detainees under the PTA may be held for up to 18 months without charge. In practice, PTA detainees are often held longer than 18 months without charge. Judges require approval from the Attorney General's Office to authorize bail for persons detained under the PTA, which the office normally did not grant. In homicide cases, regulations require the magistrate to remand the suspect, and only the High Court may grant bail. In all cases, suspects have the right to legal representation, although there is no legal provision specifically providing the right of a suspect to legal representation during interrogations in police stations and detention centers. The government provided counsel for indigent defendants in criminal cases before the High Court and courts of appeal but not in other cases; the law only required provision of counsel for cases in the High Court and courts of appeal.

On June 19, President Sirisena issued a circular setting procedures for arrests made under the PTA. The circular was developed with suggestions outlined by the HRCSL, called for detainees to be given access to legal counsel, and required detainees' families be informed of their arrests. It also banned physical harassment, torture, or humiliation of suspects; required that an arresting officer identify himself by name and rank to those arrested, and inform those arrested of the reason for the arrest; provided for access to attorneys representing the suspects; permitted only women to search female detainees; and required security forces to take prompt action to provide medical care, if needed, and adequate basic amenities. There continue to be unconfirmed reports, however, that threats, illegal detentions, torture, and abuse continued and that authorities targeted individuals involved in the transitional justice and reform process.

<u>Arbitrary Arrest</u>: According to human rights groups, the police and its Criminal Investigation and Terrorism Investigation Departments unlawfully detained people in police stations, army camps, and informal detention facilities on allegations of involvement in terrorism-related activities, without bringing charges or arraigning detainees within the timeframe required by law. Detainees were sometimes held incommunicado and lawyers had to apply for permission to meet clients, with police frequently present at such meetings. In some cases, unlawful detentions included interrogations involving mistreatment or torture. There were reports that authorities released detainees with a warning not to reveal information about their arrest or detention, under the threats of rearrest or death.

Dozens of Tamil prisoners across the country, including former LTTE cadres, undertook three hunger strikes as of October, demanding an immediate resolution to their protracted detention. As a majority of these prisoners are held under the PTA without charge, they asked the government to either indict them or provide a pathway for their eventual release.

<u>Pretrial Detention</u>: Pretrial detainees comprised half of the detainee population. The average length of time in pretrial detention was 24 hours. Lengthy legal procedures, large numbers of detainees, judicial inefficiency, and corruption often caused trial delays. Legal advocacy groups asserted it was common for the length of pretrial detention to equal or exceed the sentence for the alleged crime.

<u>Detainee's Ability to Challenge Lawfulness of Detention Before a Court</u>: Under the law, a person can challenge an arrest or detention and obtain prompt release through the courts. The legal process takes years, however, and the Center for Human Rights Development (CHRD) indicated the perceived lack of judicial independence and minimal compensation has discouraged people from seeking remedies. Under the PTA, the ability to challenge detentions is particularly limited.

e. Denial of Fair Public Trial

The law provides for an independent judiciary, and the government generally respected judicial independence.

Trial Procedures

The constitution provides for the right to a fair trial, and an independent judiciary generally enforced this right. The law presumes defendants are innocent until proven guilty. All criminal trials are public. Authorities inform defendants of the charges against them, and they have the right to counsel and the right to appeal. The government provided counsel for indigent persons tried on criminal charges in the High Court and the courts of appeal but not in cases before lower courts. Defendants have the right to confront witnesses against them, present witnesses and evidence, and access government held evidence.

The law requires court proceedings and other legislation to be available in English, Sinhala, and Tamil. Most courts outside of Jaffna and the northern and eastern parts of the country conducted business in English or Sinhala. A shortage of court appointed interpreters limited the right of Tamil speaking defendants to free interpretation as necessary, but trials and hearings in the north and east were in Tamil and English. There were few legal textbooks in Tamil. Defendants have the right to be present in court during trial and have the right to adequate time and facilities to prepare a defense. Defendants also have the right not to testify or admit guilt.

Political Prisoners and Detainees

According to CHRD, there were reports of at least 167 political prisoners; the government did not acknowledge any prisoners as political prisoners. The government permitted access to prisoners on a regular basis by the HRCSL and magistrates and gave the ICRC a limited mandate to monitor prison conditions. Authorities granted only irregular access to those providing local legal counsel, however, and conversations with clients frequently took place in the presence of police or military personnel.

Civil Judicial Procedures and Remedies

Citizens may seek civil remedies for alleged human rights violations. Individuals and organizations do not have the right to appeal domestic decisions to regional human rights bodies.

Property Restitution

Land ownership disputes between private individuals in former war zones, as well as between citizens and government entities such as the military, continued to be an issue. The Parliament unanimously passed the Prescription (Special Provisions) Act in April, which makes special legal provisions for persons who were unable to pursue their rights in court for the recovery of land due to the activities of a militant terrorist group during the period from May 1, 1983, to May 18, 2009. The Act was to remain in force for two years to resolve outstanding claims. Under previous legislation, landowners who had abandoned their land for more than 10 years forfeited their property rights, which happened to a large number of property owners displaced by the 27-year war.

The military seized significant amounts of land during the war to create security buffer zones around military bases and other high value targets, known as high security zones (HSZs). According to the 1950 Land Acquisition Act, the government may acquire private property for a "public purpose," but the law requires posting acquisition notices publicly and providing proper compensation to owners. The former government frequently posted acquisition notices for HSZ land that were inaccessible to property owners, many of whom initiated court cases, including fundamental rights cases before the Supreme Court, to challenge these acquisitions. According to the acquisition notices, most of the land acquired was for use as army camps and bases, but among the purposes listed on certain notices were the establishment of a hotel, a factory, and a farm. Throughout the year, many lawsuits, including a Supreme Court fundamental rights case and numerous writ applications filed with High Courts, remained stalled. Although there was no legal framework for HSZs following the lapse of emergency regulations in 2011, they still existed and remained off limits to civilians.

The previous government began the process of returning government occupied land to its original owners after the war ended in 2009 but the process moved slowly until the 2015 change in administration. Since January 2015, the government returned approximately 4,500 acres across several districts, including 1,055 acres near the Trincomalee Naval Base and 702 acres in the Jaffna HSZ. With the amount of land remaining to be returned to civilian owners in dispute, and with some Tamil civil society organizations arguing that it remained at approximately 13,000 acres, many of those affected by the HSZs complained that the pace at which the government demilitarized land was too slow and that the military held lands it viewed as economically valuable.

f. Arbitrary or Unlawful Interference with Privacy, Family, Home, or Correspondence

The law does not explicitly include a right to privacy. The PTA gives authority for government authorities to enter homes and monitor communications without judicial or other authorization, and there were reports the government did so. There were reports government authorities also monitored private movements without appropriate authorization.

Section 2. Respect for Civil Liberties, Including:

a. Freedom of Speech and Press

The constitution provides for freedom of speech and press and the government generally respected these rights, although there were reports government officials arrested, assaulted, and harassed journalists based on their reporting.

Freedom of Speech and Expression: The constitution provides for the right to free speech. Authorities restrict "hate speech," however, including insult to religion or religious beliefs through the Police Ordinance and Penal Code. Government authorities arrested and detained two individuals on charges of leading racial hate campaigns targeting other religious communities. Both cases are pending. The government continued to monitor political and civil society meetings, particularly in the north and east.

Press and Media Freedoms: Independent media were active and expressed a wide variety of views without restriction.

Violence and Harassment: Journalists reporting on sensitive topics were sometimes subject to arrest, physical violence, harassment, and intimidation, particularly by local police authorities.

For example, in April, journalists in Jaffna reported on a protest related to water contamination. They subsequently reported intimidation by local police authorities in an attempt to disrupt media coverage. Several of the journalists reported being followed by police, another reported threats of violence, and one was arrested.

In December, the Navy commander verbally and physically assaulted a provincial journalist during a protest at the Hambantota Port. The government issued a statement the following day saying the journalist had violated basic ethical practices while covering sensitive conflict situations.

In March the president appointed a committee to look into and seek justice for journalists subjected to harassment.

<u>Censorship or Content Restrictions</u>: The government did not directly censor the media. Journalists subject to police violence or harassment report they self-censored to avoid further harassment.

Internet Freedom

The government generally did not restrict or disrupt access to the internet or censor online content, and there were no credible reports that the government monitored private online communications without appropriate legal authority. The government placed limited restrictions on websites it deemed pornographic. Approximately 22 percent of individuals in the country use the internet, and 20 percent have access to the internet at home.

Academic Freedom and Cultural Events

The constitution provided for the freedom of assembly and association, and the government generally respected these rights. There were, however, allegations that state university officials prevented professors and university students from criticizing government officials. Some academics noted the environment of intimidation led to self-censorship.

b. Freedom of Peaceful Assembly and Association

The law provides for the freedoms of assembly and association, but the government restricted these rights in a limited number of cases.

Freedom of Assembly

The law provides for freedom of assembly, but the government did not always respect this right.

In March police used tear gas and water cannons to disperse an Inter-University Students Federation protest, after the students refused to follow police orders and started climbing over police barricades.

In July Sinhalese nationalists, allegedly aided by the police, attacked protesters from the Association to Protect the Environment and Health in Kandy.

Freedom of Association

The law provides for freedom of association but limits the right, for example by criminalizing association with or membership in banned organizations.

Evangelical churches, especially in the south, reported local government pressure and harassment to suspend worship activities that some authorities classified as "unauthorized gatherings" or to close down because they were not registered with the government.

c. Freedom of Religion

See the Department of State's *International Religious Freedom Report* at www.state.gov/religiousfreedomreport/.

d. Freedom of Movement, Internally Displaced Persons, Protection of Refugees, and Stateless Persons

The law grants every citizen "freedom of movement and of choosing his residence" and "freedom to return to the country." The government at times restricted these rights.

Abuse of Migrants, Refugees, and Stateless Persons: The government cooperated with the Office of the UN High Commissioner for Refugees (UNHCR) and other humanitarian organizations in providing protection and assistance to internally displaced persons (IDPs), refugees, returning refugees, stateless persons, or other persons of concern.

Foreign Travel: The government imposed an overseas travel ban on human rights activist Balendran Jeyakumari for an indefinite period.

Internally Displaced Persons

The country's long civil war that ended in 2009 caused widespread, prolonged displacement, including forced displacement by the government and LTTE, particularly of Tamils. According to the government's Ministry of Resettlement,

Rehabilitation, Hindu Religious Affairs, and Prison Reforms, 43,607 citizens remained IDPs as of August 31. The large majority resided in Jaffna, Kilinochchi, Puttalam, and Trincomalee districts in the north and east. While all IDPs had full freedom of movement, most were unable to return home due to uncleared land mines; restrictions designating their home areas as part of HSZs or exclusive economic zones; lack of work opportunities; inability to access basic public services, including acquiring documents verifying land ownership; and lack of government resolution of competing land claims and other war related destruction. The government did not provide protection and assistance to IDPs in welfare camps.

The government promoted the return and resettlement of IDPs by returning military seized land and making state land available for landless IDPs. In August the government approved a national policy on durable solutions for conflict affected displacement to provide a rights based set of principles and standards to guide all stakeholders working with IDPs and displaced populations, in accordance with law and policy and international law and humanitarian standards. The military and other government agencies supported the resettlement of IDPs by constructing houses, schools, toilets, and providing other social services on recently released lands.

Protection of Refugees

<u>Access to Asylum</u>: The law does not provide for the granting of asylum or refugee status. The government relied on UNHCR to provide food, housing, and education for refugees in the country and to pursue third-country resettlement for them. Refugees and asylum seekers are not legally permitted to work or enroll in the government school system, but many worked informally.

Section 3. Freedom to Participate in the Political Process

The constitution provides citizens the ability to choose their government in free and fair periodic elections held by secret ballot and based on universal and equal suffrage.

Elections and Political Participation

<u>Recent Elections</u>: The Commonwealth Observer Group reported that voters in the January 2015 presidential election were able to exercise their franchise freely and that vote counting was transparent, with the results swiftly revealed to the public.

Observers reported widespread abuse of state resources used for campaigning, consistent bias in state media toward the former government, and denial of access to venues for the opposition candidate.

Domestic and international observers concurred that the August 2015 parliamentary elections were conducted in a fair and free manner with few reports of violence. The European Union election observation mission's preliminary findings stated that the elections were "well administered and offered voters a genuine choice from among a broad range of political alternatives, although campaign rules were restrictive." The mission added that freedoms of assembly and movement were respected and that, despite restrictive campaign rules, such as not allowing candidates to engage in door-to-door campaigning, canvass in person, or distribute leaflets, party activists and candidates campaigned vigorously.

Participation of Women and Minorities: There are no laws that prevent women or minorities from participating in political life on the same basis as men or majority citizens.

Section 4. Corruption and Lack of Transparency in Government

The law provides criminal penalties for corruption by officials, and the government began to implement the law effectively but remained constrained by a lack of technical expertise and resources. Officials in various branches of government engaged in corrupt practices, albeit under a heightened level of scrutiny. There were numerous reports of government corruption.

Corruption: Corruption remained an issue. A parliamentary panel, the Committee on Public Enterprises, launched an investigation against then central bank governor Arjuna Mahendran amid allegations that Mahendran had given his son-in-law insider information and they had both benefited from sovereign bond sales. Mahendran has also been accused of multimillion rupee spending on his government credit card. Mahendran has denied the allegations and an earlier investigation cleared him. The government has yet to take action against Mahendran, despite the parliamentary panel's conclusion in October that Mahendran acted improperly.

Financial Disclosure: The law requires all candidates for parliamentary, local government, provincial, and presidential elections to declare their assets and liabilities to the speaker of parliament. Some candidates in parliamentary elections published their financial reports, but there was no enforcement of the law against those who did not. By law, members of the public may access records relating to the assets and liabilities of elected officials by paying a fee.

Public Access to Information: A law passed in June provides for public access to government information, and the law is set to come into effect on February 3, 2017.

Section 5. Governmental Attitude Regarding International and Nongovernmental Investigation of Alleged Violations of Human Rights

A number of domestic and international human rights groups investigated and published their findings on human rights cases.

Government Human Rights Bodies: The HRCSL has jurisdiction to inquire into human rights violations. After an allegation is established, the HRCSL may recommend financial compensation; refer the case for disciplinary action or to the attorney general for prosecution, or both, with presidential approval. If the government does not follow an HRCSL order, a summons may be sent to both parties for explanation. If the parties continue in noncompliance, the HRCSL may report the case to the High Court as contempt, an offense punishable by imprisonment or fine. By statute the HRCSL has wide powers and resources and may not be called as a witness in any court of law or be sued for matters relating to its official duties. Senior HRCSL officers reported that the HRCSL continued to suffer from staffing shortages but hired additional employees to help reduce the backlog of cases.

Section 6. Discrimination, Societal Abuses, and Trafficking in Persons

Women

Rape and Domestic Violence: The law prohibits rape and domestic violence, but enforcement of the law was inconsistent. The prescribed penalties for rape are seven to 20 years' imprisonment and a fine of at least 200,000 thousand rupees (Rs) ($1,333); for domestic violence, a victim can obtain a protection order for one year and request a maintenance allowance. The law only prohibits spousal rape if the spouses are separated legally. Sexual assault, rape, and spousal abuse are pervasive societal problems.

Many women's organizations believed that greater sensitization of police and the judiciary was necessary to make progress in combating rape. The police Bureau for the Prevention of Abuse of Women and Children conducted awareness programs in schools and at the grassroots level to encourage women to file complaints. Police continued to establish women's units in police stations.

Services to assist survivors of rape and domestic violence, such as crisis centers, legal aid, and counseling, were generally scarce nationwide due to a lack of funding. Language barriers between service providers and victims also were reported in the north and east, where Tamil speaking victims lacked access to Tamil speaking service providers. There was one government established shelter for victims of domestic violence. The Ministry of Health, in partnership with nongovernmental organizations (NGOs), maintained hospital based centers to provide medical assistance to those requiring attention for sexual assault related injuries before referral to legal and psychosocial services.

Sexual Harassment: Sexual harassment is a criminal offense carrying a maximum sentence of five years in prison. Sexual harassment was common. In October, the National Police Commission decided to designate senior female law enforcement officers for every province to respond to sexual harassment claims.

The Supreme Court found in October in favor of a schoolteacher who went public with her claims of sexual harassment after school authorities did not take any action on her claim. The schoolteacher gave an interview to the media about her views on the official inquiry, although public officers are not permitted to disclose information on internal disciplinary matters. The court found that the continued sexual harassment and inaction on her case and her need to express this suffering outweighed the rules on disclosing information.

Reproductive Rights: Couples and individuals have the right to decide the number, spacing, and timing of their children; manage their reproductive health; and have access to the information and means to do so, free from discrimination, coercion, or violence.

Discrimination: Women have equal rights under civil and criminal law. Adjudication of questions related to family law--including marriage, divorce, child custody, and inheritance--varied according to the customary law of each ethnic or religious group, resulting in discrimination. The Muslim Marriage and Divorce Act permits girls to marry at age 12, in contrast to the civil law, which sets the minimum marital age at 18 and the minimum age of sexual consent at 16. According to Tamil civil society groups in the Northern Province, marriages are governed by civil law, while the Thesawalamai customary law governs the division of property.

Children

Birth Registration: Children obtain citizenship from their parents. Authorities generally registered births immediately, and failure to register resulted in denial of some public services, such as education.

Child Abuse: Although there are no available government or NGO statistics on child abuse, there were reports of sexual abuse of children by teachers, school principals, and religious instructors, as well as a number of child rape cases in which government officials were the suspected perpetrators. Civil society organizations working on children's issues asserted there were insufficient mechanisms for children to report domestic violence or abuse safely. Although police stations are supposed to have an officer dedicated to handling abuse complaints from women and children, this was not consistently implemented throughout the country. During the reporting period, the government cooperated with UNICEF to run a social media campaign highlighting online safety and violence against women and children.

Early and Forced Marriage: The minimum legal age for marriage is 18 for both men and women, although girls may marry at age 16 with parental consent. The Ministry of Women and Children's Affairs conducted programs in many districts to educate the public at the village level on the complications that may result from early marriage. According to the penal code, sexual intercourse with a girl below 16 years of age, with or without her consent, amounts to statutory rape. The provision, however, does not apply to married Muslim girls above the age of 12.

Sexual Exploitation of Children: The law prohibits the commercial sexual exploitation of children, the sale of children, offering or procuring a child for child prostitution, and practices related to child pornography, but authorities did not always enforce the law. The minimum age of consensual sex was 16. According to UNICEF, children under age 18 from conflict affected zones, tea estate regions, and poor rural areas were widely engaged in prostitution.

Child sex tourism remained a problem.

Displaced Children: Children in IDP welfare centers and relocation sites were exposed to the same difficult conditions as adult IDPs and returnees in these areas.

<u>International Child Abductions</u>: The country is a party to the 1980 Hague Convention on the Civil Aspects of International Child Abduction. See the Department of State's *Annual Report on Parental Child Abduction* at travel.state.gov/content/childabduction/en/legal/compliance.html.

Anti-Semitism

The Jewish population remained very small. There were no reports of anti-Semitic acts.

Trafficking in Persons

See the Department of State's *Trafficking in Persons Report* at www.state.gov/j/tip/rls/tiprpt/.

Persons with Disabilities

Various laws forbid discrimination against any person with physical, sensory, intellectual, or mental disabilities in employment, education, air travel, other public transportation, and access to health care. In practice, however, discrimination occurred in employment, education, and provision of state services, including public transportation. Children with disabilities attended school at a lower rate than other persons. There were regulations on accessibility, but accommodation for access to buildings and public transportation for persons with disabilities was rare. There were no regulations guaranteeing access to information and communications.

National/Racial/Ethnic Minorities

Both local and Indian origin Tamils maintained they suffered longstanding, systematic discrimination in university education, government employment, housing, health services, language laws, and procedures for naturalization of noncitizens. Tamils throughout the country, but especially in the north and east, reported security forces regularly monitored or harassed members of their community, especially young and middle-aged Tamil men.

The government had a variety of ministries and presidentially appointed bodies designed to address the social and development needs of the Tamil minority. The primary entities were the Ministry of Resettlement, Rehabilitation, and Hindu

Religious Affairs and Prison Reforms and the Ministry of Upcountry New Villages, Estate Infrastructure, and Community Development, both headed by ethnic Tamils.

The government has implemented a number of confidence building measures to address grievances of the Tamil community. It has replaced military governors of the Northern and Eastern provinces with former diplomats and seasoned civil servants.

The Office of National Unity and Reconciliation, established by the president, coordinated the government's reconciliation efforts. Its four main focus areas were promoting social integration to build an inclusive society, securing language rights for all citizens, supporting a healing process within war affected communities via the government's proposed Commission for Truth, Justice, Reconciliation and Nonrecurrence, and providing coordinated development planning for war affected regions.

The Muslim community constitutes the third largest ethnic and religious group in the country, accounting for 9.7 percent of the population. There were reports of occasional attacks on Muslims and their property, especially by Sinhalese, for their distinct cultural and religious practices in dress, food, and lifestyle.

Indigenous People

The country's indigenous people, known as Veddas, reportedly numbered fewer than 1,000. Some preferred to maintain their traditional way of life, and the law nominally protected them. There were no legal restrictions on their participation in political or economic life, but lack of legal documents was a problem for many. Vedda communities complained that the creation of protected forest areas pushed them off their lands and deprived them of traditional livelihoods.

Acts of Violence, Discrimination, and Other Abuses Based on Sexual Orientation and Gender Identity

Three legal statutes constitute the architecture for discrimination against lesbian, gay, bisexual, transgender, and intersex (LGBTI) persons in the country: Section 365(A) of the penal code, which criminalizes acts "against the order of nature"; Section 399 of this code regarding "Cheating by Personation"; and the Vagrancy Ordinance. Section 365(A), although lacking clear legal definition, puts those convicted of engaging in same-sex sexual activity in private or in public at risk of

10 years' imprisonment. Antidiscrimination laws prohibited discrimination based on sex but did not prohibit discrimination based on sexual orientation and gender identity.

UN human rights officials noted that police used the Vagrancy Ordinance to detain transgender individuals on suspicion they were engaging in prostitution. Police used Section 399 to harass persons who expressed themselves in gender nonconforming ways on grounds of "impersonation." Criminal prosecutions under these statues were rare, however. Human rights organizations reported that police targeted LGBTI individuals for assault, harassment, and monetary and sexual extortion.

Transgender persons continued to face discrimination and abuse, including arbitrary detention, mistreatment, and discrimination accessing employment, housing, and health care. In August the government approved the issuance of gender recognition certificates by consultant psychiatrists, which would enable transgender individuals at various stages in the gender reassignment process to amend their gender on government issued identity documents. One transgender individual alleged persons from her community could apply for new government issued identity documents only after having undergone a full course of sexual reassignment surgery.

A Sinhala nationalist group known as "The Island Nation of Sinhale" (Lion's Blood) threatened and insulted the organizers of Colombo PRIDE 2016 on Facebook.

HIV and AIDS Social Stigma

There were reports of discrimination against persons who provided HIV prevention services and against groups at high risk of infection. For example, there are reports hospital officials publicize the HIV positive status of their clients and occasionally refuse to provide healthcare to HIV positive persons. In an April 28 decision, the Supreme Court issued a directive prohibiting HIV discrimination in education in a case in which the school system had denied entry to a student based on a rumor he was HIV-positive. The court held that the constitutional mandate of universal access to education requires that children living with or affected by HIV must have such access. The court further outlined the state's obligation to take necessary measures to protect, promote, and respect the human rights of persons living with HIV.

Other Societal Violence or Discrimination

Sources stated some Buddhist monks regularly tried to close down Christian and Muslim places of worship on the grounds they lacked the Ministry of Justice and Buddha Sasana's approval. The National Christian Evangelical Alliance of Sri Lanka documented a total of 77 cases of attacks on churches, intimidation and violence against pastors and their congregations, and obstruction of worship services as of October 31.

Section 7. Worker Rights

a. Freedom of Association and the Right to Collective Bargaining

The law provides for the right of workers to form and join unions of their choice, with the exception of members of the armed forces, police officers, judicial officers, and prison officers. Workers in nonessential services industries, except for workers in public service unions, have the legal right to bargain collectively.

Under Emergency Regulations of the Public Security Ordinance, the president has broad discretion to declare sectors "essential" to national security, the life of the community, or the preservation of public order. In 2011 the government lifted the emergency regulations. The law prohibits retribution against strikers in nonessential sectors. Seven workers may form a union, adopt a charter, elect leaders, and publicize their views, but a union must represent 40 percent of workers at a given enterprise before the law legally obligates the employer to bargain with the union. The law does not permit public sector unions to form federations or represent workers from more than one branch or department of government. The Labor Ministry may cancel a union's registration if it fails to submit an annual report for three years.

The law prohibits antiunion discrimination. Labor laws do not cover domestic workers employed in the homes of others or informal sector workers.

The law allows unions to conduct their activities without interference, but the government enforced the law unevenly. Violations for antiunion discrimination may result in a fine of 100,000 Rs ($666). The law requires an employer found guilty of antiunion discrimination to reinstate workers fired for union activities, but it may transfer them to different locations. These penalties generally were not sufficient to deter violations. Only the Labor Ministry has legal standing to pursue an unfair labor practice case, including for antiunion discrimination.

Since 1999 the Labor Ministry had filed only nine cases against companies for unfair labor practices under the Industrial Disputes Act. As of September 2015, the courts had concluded two cases and continued to try the other seven. The courts did not add any cases during the year. Citing routine government inaction on alleged violations of labor rights, some unions pressed for standing to sue, while some smaller unions did not want that ability, citing the cost of filing cases. Workers brought some labor violations to court under Termination of Employment and Workmen Act and Payment of Gratuity Act. Judicial procedures were subject to lengthy delays. The Industrial Dispute Act does not apply to the public sector, and there was no formal dispute resolution mechanism for public sector unions.

Freedom of association and the right to bargain collectively were generally, but not always, respected. Union activists and officials remained subject to harassment, intimidation, and other retaliatory practices. Employers arbitrarily transferred or unfairly dismissed union members.

While some unions in the public sector were politically independent, most large unions affiliated with political parties and played a prominent role in the political process.

Unions alleged that employers often indefinitely delayed recognition of unions to avoid collective bargaining, decrease support for unionization, or identify, terminate, and sometimes assault or threaten union activists. To address these concerns, the ministry issued a circular in 2011 requiring labor commissioners to hold union certification elections within 30 working days of an application for registration if there was no objection, or within 45 working days if there was an objection. Information regarding the number of elections was unavailable.

b. Prohibition of Forced or Compulsory Labor

The law prohibits all forms of forced and compulsory labor, but penalties were not sufficient to deter violations. The government generally enforced the laws, but resources, inspections, and remediation efforts were not adequate. Labor Ministry inspections did not extend to domestic workers. There were reports of sporadic government prosecutions of labor agents who fraudulently recruited migrant workers, and the government appeared to sustain past efforts to enhance interministerial coordination through monthly meetings.

Children between the ages of 14 and 18 and women working as live-in domestic workers in some homes were vulnerable to forced labor.

Also see the Department of State's *Trafficking in Persons Report* at www.state.gov/j/tip/rls/tiprpt/.

c. Prohibition of Child Labor and Minimum Age for Employment

The minimum age for employment is 14, although the law permits the employment of younger children by their parents or guardians in limited family agricultural work or technical training. The law prohibits hazardous work for persons under age 18. The law limits the working hours of children ages 14 and 15 to nine hours per day and of ages 16 and 17 to 10 hours per day. The government did not effectively enforce all laws and penalties were not sufficient to deter violations.

The Labor Ministry made some progress in implementing its plan to eliminate the worst forms of child labor by the end of the year. For example, the government declared all 25 districts of the country as "child labor free zones" as part of its declared commitment to eradicate hazardous child labor nationwide. District officials, including education officials in the districts, were educated on hazardous child labor, and the Department of Labor strengthened its efforts to monitor workplaces on the list of hazardous work for children. The ministry cited lack of funds for the full implementation of the plan.

Agriculture was the largest sector employing child labor, both legally and illegally. Children worked both in plantations and in nonplantation agriculture during harvest periods. In addition to agriculture, children worked as street vendors, domestic helpers, and in the mining, construction, manufacturing, transport, and fishing industries. Children displaced by the war were especially vulnerable to employment in hazardous labor.

Several thousands of children between ages 14 and 18 were employed in domestic service in urban households. There are no laws regulating employment in third-party households, including the employment of children. Employers reportedly subjected child domestic workers to physical, sexual, and emotional abuse; observers also reported rural children in debt bondage in urban households. Child employment was also common in family enterprises, such as family farms, crafts, small trade establishments, restaurants, and repair shops. Criminals exploited children, especially boys, in prostitution in coastal areas as part of sex tourism (see section 6, Children).

Also see the Department of Labor's *Findings on the Worst Forms of Child Labor* at www.dol.gov/ilab/reports/child-labor/findings/.

d. Discrimination with Respect to Employment and Occupation

The constitution prohibits discrimination, including with respect to employment and occupation, on the basis of race, religion, language, caste, sex, political opinion, or place of birth. The law did not prohibit discrimination with respect to employment and occupation on the basis of color, sexual orientation and/or gender identity, age, HIV positive status, or status with regard to other communicable diseases.

The government did not effectively enforce these laws and discrimination occurred based on the above categories with respect to employment and occupation. Some institutions would regularly specify particular positions as requiring male or female recruits. Women had no legal protection against discrimination and were sometimes paid less than men for equal work.

There were reports of discrimination based on HIV/AIDS status in which persons lost their jobs. There were two national policies on HIV/AIDS, but there were no laws to protect HIV/AIDS affected persons in the workplace.

e. Acceptable Conditions of Work

The Parliament passed its first-ever national minimum wage law in March that mandated a wage of 10,000 Rs ($66) per month and 400 Rs ($2.69) per day. In addition, 44 wage boards established by the Department of Labor continued to set minimum wages and working conditions by sector and industry, in consultation with unions and employers. Private sector workers receiving a monthly wage less than 40,000 Rs ($266) were given a government mandated salary increase of 2,500 Rs ($16) per month under a budgetary relief allowance law passed by Parliament in March. During the year the minimum wage in the public sector increased to 32,040 Rs ($214) from 31,876 Rs ($212) in 2015 and 21,876 Rs ($146) in 2014. As of November 2015, the official estimate of the poverty income level was 4,038 Rs ($27) per person per month, although some analysts questioned the validity of this estimate.

The law prohibits most full time workers from regularly working more than 45 hours per week (a five-and-a-half-day workweek). In addition, the law stipulates a rest period of one hour per day. Regulations limit the maximum overtime hours to 15 per week. Overtime pay is 1.5 times the basic wage and is paid for work done on Sundays or holidays. The provision limiting basic work hours is not applicable to managers and executives in a public institution. The law provides for paid annual holidays.

The government sets occupational health and safety standards. Workers have the right to remove themselves from dangerous situations, but many workers were unaware of such rights or feared that they would lose their jobs if they did so.

Authorities did not effectively enforce minimum wage, hours of work, and occupational safety and health standards in all sectors. The Labor Ministry's resources, inspections, and remediation efforts were inadequate. Occupational health and safety standards in the rapidly growing construction sector, including on infrastructure development projects, such as port, airport, and road construction, as well as high-rise buildings, were insufficient. There was a growing trend, particularly in the construction industry, for employers to use contract employment for work of a regular nature, and contract workers had fewer safeguards.

Labor Ministry inspectors checked whether employers were providing complete pay to employees and were contributing to pension funds as required by law, but unions questioned whether the inspections were effective. During the year, the Labor Department deployed a computerized Labor Information System Application designed eventually to improve the efficiency and effectiveness of inspections was still at its very early stages. The financial punishment for nonpayment of wages and pension contributions is negligible, with fines ranging from 100 Rs ($0.66) to 250 Rs ($1.66) for the first offense and 500 Rs ($3.33) to 1,000 Rs ($6.66), incarceration for a term of six months for the third offense, or both. The penalties for violation of hours of work laws under the Shop and Office Act are a fine of 500 Rs ($3.33), six months imprisonment, or both. The law charges a fine of 50 Rs ($0.33) per day if the offense continues after conviction. These penalties were not sufficient to deter violations. Labor inspectors did not monitor wages or working conditions or provide programs or social protections for informal sector workers, of which there were significant numbers.

There were no reliable sources of data for the informal sector and no government agency that tracked industrial or workplace accidents.

www.ingramcontent.com/pod-product-compliance
Lightning Source LLC
Chambersburg PA
CBHW080820280726
48660CB00018B/3556